Lessons Learned
ON BISHOP STREET

LESSONS LEARNED
ON BISHOP STREET

LOCAL VALUES FOR ISLAND BUSINESS

WESLEY T. PARK

WATERMARK
PUBLISHING

ISBN 0-9779143-3-X

Library of Congress Control Number:
2006933791

Design and production
Maggie Fujino

For special corporate discounts and
other bulk orders of this book, contact
the publisher directly or use the order
form on page 174.

Watermark Publishing
1088 Bishop Street, Suite 310
Honolulu, HI 96813

TELEPHONE: Toll-free 1-866-900-BOOK
WEB SITE: www.bookshawaii.net
EMAIL: sales@bookshawaii.net

Printed in the United States

As a youngster I admired the tough "Bulls of Bethel Street."

As a working man I admire the brilliant "Bulls of Bishop Street":
John Bellinger, Herbert Cornuelle, Robert Pfeiffer, Masayuki Tokioka.
Sam Cooke, Walter Dods, Duane Kurisu and Duncan MacNaughton.

Sometimes I wish I was smart like them
instead of better looking.

ABOUT THE AUTHOR

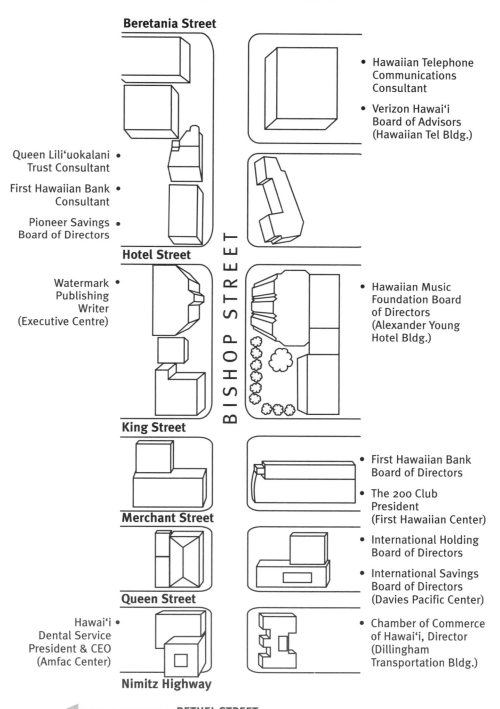

Beretania Street

- Hawaiian Telephone Communications Consultant
- Verizon Hawai'i Board of Advisors (Hawaiian Tel Bldg.)

Queen Lili'uokalani Trust Consultant

First Hawaiian Bank Consultant

Pioneer Savings Board of Directors

Hotel Street

Watermark Publishing Writer (Executive Centre)

- Hawaiian Music Foundation Board of Directors (Alexander Young Hotel Bldg.)

BISHOP STREET

King Street

- First Hawaiian Bank Board of Directors
- The 200 Club President (First Hawaiian Center)

Merchant Street

- International Holding Board of Directors
- International Savings Board of Directors (Davies Pacific Center)

Queen Street

Hawai'i Dental Service President & CEO (Amfac Center)

- Chamber of Commerce of Hawai'i, Director (Dillingham Transportation Bldg.)

Nimitz Highway

← **BETHEL STREET**
Two Blocks and Three Lifetimes away

INTRODUCTION

Many of the values that our friends and my wife, Daphne, and I have as adults are the result of what we first learned as children in Hawai'i's public school system. Following are excerpts from a talk that I presented to the Public Schools Foundation on May 17, 2005.

"Memories of Public School

In public school there were so many different kinds of people that being different was no big thing.

There were some real geniuses—and some guys who had hard time adding and subtracting. Some rich, some poor, some strong, some weak. All different races, religions, kamaainas and malihinis, all different kinds of disabilities and people with all different kinds of special talents.

But when I think about it I realized that everybody was good at something.

Even though we were all different, this is what we had in common:

• Respect for the Hawaiian culture

• Pidgin English (for example, in every house when your father said "Gonfonnit" in a loud voice, you knew it was time to go have dinner at your neighbor's house)

• Feelings were very, very important to all of us. You could hit a local boy with a baseball bat and he wouldn't cry, but if you hurt his feelings he might.

On the School Playground: Learning the Local Ways

We learned to love our close friends unequivocally and for life, with loyalty—right or wrong, whether they were up or down. We learned not to take ourselves too seriously but to take our close friendships very seriously. We learned to make close friends one at a time, not by joining a group or gang. We learned that if someone didn't like you, you should not try to be his or her friend; you should just stay away.

We learned that some relationships were just situational, where you just happened to be in the same place at the same time. When the situation changed, we lost the closeness. Some people will feel that they have outgrown you. But even though their love turned out to be temporary, it was OK to love them more than they loved you—as long as you didn't make a fool of yourself. As we used to say: "No make A!"

As time went on, however, we learned that we cannot spend all our time trying not to "make A." We learned to try instead to establish new goals and achievements. We learned that to try and still not be the best, or even to be lousy, was *not* "make A" as long as we did our very best. Doing your very best was the most important thing. As we used to say, sometimes you gotta chance 'um and you gotta geeve 'um.

Learning to Tell The Difference in Life Between Form and Substance

Greasy long hair, a cigarette in the mouth, and stink eye was form. Substance was having moral courage—the courage to say and act the way you believed in, under any circumstances, and to accept the consequences with grace and dignity.

Speaking the King's English all the time was form. Substance was the ability to communicate with logic and to find solutions to problems.

We learned to pick substance over form. As we used to say to the "formy" people: "No act!"

Some Lessons Learned in Public School Classrooms

We learned to *read*.

We learned not to believe everything we read.

We learned to compare what we were reading to other things we read, saw or heard.

We learned to let fiction take us to faraway places and faraway times and to multiply our own experiences by facing make-believe situations.

We learned to read with our minds as well as with our eyes.

When writing, we were taught to "express," not to "impress."

We learned to appreciate art—the colors, shapes, forms, composition and skills of the artists. Best of all, we developed our own tastes.

We learned to appreciate music—the melodies and harmonies, the skills of the instrumentalists, the talents of the singers and the blending of beautiful sounds.

We learned to enjoy music not only with our ears, but also with our hearts.

We learned to enjoy reading, to appreciate art and to appreciate music from our public school teachers, and these joys turned out to be joys of a lifetime."

In Hawai'i, the work culture is constantly evolving to embrace new people and new ideas. The values and codes of behavior that we learned in school have a lasting effect on that culture, as these lessons are constantly applied in our professional lives. Our challenge is to bring in new ideas that improve our work environment, without overpowering our time-honored basic local values.

With Aloha,
Wesley T. Park

Management concepts are very easy to read and understand, but they are very difficult to practice consistently because very often ego, selfishness and false pride get in the way.

In business, money is the ultimate scoreboard.

Determination of whether you win or lose in the end will depend on what is on this scoreboard.

Don't take yourself too seriously.

Have fun, be able to laugh at
yourself but take your responsibilities
deadly serious.

Do not focus only on the process.

Instead, focus first on getting
positive results.

What we are today is a sum total of everything that has happened to us and how we reacted.

React positively every day to become a winner, not only now but also in the future.

Before you interview for a job make
sure that you learn about the company.
Use annual reports, the Internet and
ask people you know.

Because the particular job you apply
for is only as good as the company is,
and if the company fails, you fail.

In Hawaii a racial reference is not important per se, it is simply a form of identification; pay attention only to how it is being used and the adjective used before the race.

Better yet, don't pay attention to race because it's the culture, not the race, that gives us the values that we live by.

When buying property, make sure you walk on the land first—at high tide.

Think of positive solutions for
the company and move forward.

Never panic or get paralyzed with
fear for yourself.

When you say you're going to do
something, do it no matter how minor;
otherwise you will be known as
a bullshitter.

But if you cannot or do not want to
do it, say so up front.

If you tried and cannot do it, say so.

Don't filter and censor information to your boss to further your own cause.

State the facts and point out your opinions separately.

Surround yourself with people who will tell you the truth, because the quality of your decisions will depend on the facts that you have before you.

"That's the way it is" is not acceptable, because it is an indicator that nothing is going to change or get better.

Do the right thing for your company
no matter what the naysayers say.

Negative people who play games
always get in the way of progress.

People who make progress always
overcome negativity with positive
thinking and guts.

Even if the immediate consequences are painful, do the right thing for the long run.

Constantly ask yourself:
Are you solving the problem or
are you adding to the problem?

Bringing structure to an organization
brings a semblance of order.

The structure not only has to look
good on paper but must work with
real people.

Always close the loop:
<u>get information back</u> to whomever
requests action, makes complaints
or makes suggestions.

People who kiss up to people
higher on the ladder fut down on
people below them on the ladder.

These people think it's OK
because they think their futs
smell like perfume.

Keep your word, because you will see the same people over and over again when you're on an island.

So don't give your word unless you're really sure that you can keep it.

Break up your big problems into steps,
solve them one step at a time and
<u>enjoy the solutions</u> at each step.

Listen to everybody, because even
a_ _ _ _ _s have good ideas sometimes.

When something goes wrong or doesn't go the way it's supposed to, don't start defending yourself or blaming others.

Instead, 1) identify the problem, 2) mass resources to fix the problem, and 3) determine how to prevent the problem from happening again.

People who are not nice don't know how to be nice, but they are very envious of the aloha that nice people get from others.

Being on time for meetings, meeting deadlines, and keeping promises to perform are often used as factors to initially judge people's competency.

To be on time you have to learn how
to end meetings before the next one is
scheduled to begin.

When you hire, remember that people of poor character will have a negative impact on your company no matter how much talent they possess, and they will often cause more problems than they are worth.

Don't react on your first instinct.

Many times first instincts are more
personal rather than professional
in nature.

Leaders multiply their skills by
developing skills in others.

Train people starting at their present level of knowledge, because if there is a gap between what they know and what you are trying to teach them, confusion will reign.

Systems are only as good as people
are trained to use them.

No sense in having sophisticated
systems with nobody who can
utilize them.

You must embrace change with a positive attitude in order to advance and improve.

Fighting change will not only cause you to fail professionally but will also cause you to be unhappy personally.

Training and learning must be
continuous in order for people and
companies to move forward and
be competitive.

Technological change can be revolutionary but changes in corporate culture are always evolutionary.

Company bullies often make the mistake of thinking that niceness is a weakness.

When bullies cross the line you must avoid them, let them know that they are being a pain, or smash 'um. (Remember, you have to accept the consequences.)

Give your employees a chance by supporting them effectively and decisively.

Bring respect to your position by being professional and competent.

Being liked is a bonus.

Plan ahead, because if you don't know where you are going you won't know when you are headed over a cliff.

Employees can only be as good as
you allow them to be, because it is
very difficult to be successful in a
dysfunctional setting.

From time to time go back to basics to reestablish a common base to work from. Even though everyone might understand the basics, many often must be reminded to apply them.

Listen to complaints, because you
can look at them as opportunities
to discover problems and to prevent
problems from happening in the future.

Treat each person as a human being who deserves to be treated with care and respect. Just remember that everyone is somebody's child.

No matter how well you think you are doing you should always strive for improvement.

Your competitors are working hard to be better, for sure.

Cutting jobs only through attrition usually results in hard personnel decisions being deferred and an uneven distribution of work.

Companies should review all of their departments with an eye on fair distribution of resources as the next step.

Nothing great is accomplished without enthusiasm, focus and hard work.

Personal and professional development
allows us to have choices in the future.

Better yourself now for your present
duties and you will automatically
be preparing yourself for further
opportunities in the future.

Respect has to be earned.

The basis for earning respect is self–respect and respect for others.

We need to constantly show respect
for others by listening and paying
attention to their problems

But remember, most of us are not
social workers.

As a leader it is not only what you produce but, more important, what others produce with you that matters.

We cannot do all things at one time.
We need to set priorities, allocate
resources and move ahead one step
at a time with the big picture always
in sight.

The company is a collective reflection of what each of us contributes.

Therefore, the accomplishments of every single employee are very important.

Don't talk overly loud to a local unless you are speaking to a deaf person.

In order to do the big things right, you
have to do the small things right first.

In meetings speak when you have
something positive to contribute.
Never speak up just to shine.

Use payday as a reminder to be
thankful for having your job, because
you could easily be worse off than
you are now.

On the island of Hawaii do not buy
property with warm lava on it.

Never allow yourself to join up with weaklings against people who think big or outside the box.

As you advance in your career, do not ever think that you are better than the people below you.

Never forget that they helped to make you successful.

People in Hawaii are often referred to
by their high school or their race.

Every company must have a clear
mission statement, not only for its
board and executives, but also one that
is understood by all of the employees.

It is helpful to create an internal theme for every stage of endeavor, in order for the company to set the tone for the next big push.

All companies must match up the skills and attitudes of each and every employee with the needs of the company at every stage.

Give praise to those who are contributing, and give training and counseling to those who are not.

Do not wait until you're angry to correct employees who are not doing good work or who are not getting along with others.

Have a system where employees are given an opportunity to improve by correcting shortcomings or flaws early, before emotions set in.

But be sure that you do not appear to be nitpicking.

Bosses should remember that whenever
they fire someone, everyone else is
wondering who is going to be next
(the best workers as well as the
not– so–good ones).

When excellent workers are unhappy they will find another good job.

The ordinary ones often have no place better to go.

Bosses often just move unproductive
workers around or give them less
work, because the bosses don't have
the ability to train or the guts to get rid
of them if they are not trainable.

This creates a heavy burden on the
good workers who have to pick up
the slack.

Bosses should always remember to give praise whenever praise is due.

Better yet, bosses should say thanks publicly when good work is done.

In business, people who brag that they "have it made" usually are out of a job shortly thereafter.

Stealing pencils for personal use
and stealing money from the company
are both stealing.

Thieves have a mindset that has no
respect for the company's ownership
of property.

Be friendly and caring to the people who work for you.

Be aware that a few people will try to take advantage; keep them at arm's length.

But don't let the very few uncaring individuals make you forget how terrific the others are.

When hiring outside consultants, be sure that you and they know and agree on exactly what is expected in terms of <u>results</u> before they start.

Negotiate all costs with consultants in writing before they start, but only after the scope of work and the expected results are determined.

Set sub-goals, schedules and reports
so that you don't find out too late that
your company is off course.

When planning fiscal turnarounds
also appraise the effects on
production, employee relations
and customer relations.

Successful bosses not only have to have a driving <u>will to succeed</u> but they must convey this strong will to their employees by their actions as well as their words.

This is especially true when things are not going right.

Employees must feel that their leader believes in himself and the employees to make the company succeed.

In business, <u>communication</u> is so important that it must be built into the structure.

Provisions must be made not only for what you communicate, but also how and when you communicate, with each constituent group—the Board, management, employees, unions, customers, vendors, media, regulatory agencies, lawyers and accountants.

Businesses should look outside
themselves whenever a lack of
resources is a problem.

Partnering not only with other
businesses but with community groups
with common goals sometimes provides
a critical mass of resources, not only
fiscally but also in terms of knowledge,
relationships with other groups and
political contacts.

All consultants want the whole consulting package, but sometimes it's better to break out some portions for which expert specialists are available.

But if you break up a consulting package, pay special attention to coordination right from the start.

Management information systems
must be regularly reviewed for quality
due to constant external technical
changes, and, more important, to be sure
that they are meeting changing needs
for information.

When you continually make adjustments
to a system you have to ensure that
you don't end up with an uncoordinated
patchwork system.

A company should review management
structures on a regular basis to ensure
that as the company's needs change
it has enough decision makers and
managers with the right expertise,
and doesn't have any deadwood.

One-time windfall profits should not be used for new programs without careful consideration of the increased income that will be required for years to come to match the increased costs.

Many times companies take comfort
in increases in sales volume without
enough consideration of profit per
unit and expenses.

When you need cash, you can either
earn more or spend less.

It's easier to spend less than to
earn more.

Executives should use lawyers for advice on legal matters and accountants for advice on accounting matters, period.

Executives have the responsibility to make business decisions and should not try to pass their responsibilities to their lawyers or accountants.

Long-time vendor contracts should be reviewed and re-bid periodically to ensure fair pricing.

(Especially if the president's wife's brother is one of the vendors.)

Management and labor unions have one huge responsibility in common: The people who are the company's employees and are, at the same time, members of the union.

Contribute to your company so that when you leave you will feel that the company is a little better for your having been there.

PAU

One Good *Lesson* Deserves Another

 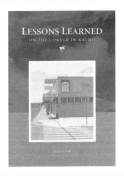

NAME: _____

ADDRESS: _____

CITY/STATE/ZIP: _____

PHONE: _____

EMAIL: _____

Lessons Learned on the Corner in Kalihi:

$12.95 x _____ = $ _____

Lessons Learned on Bishop Street:

$12.95 x _____ = $ _____

Shipping and Handling: $5 for the first book $ 5.00

$2 ea. add'l book $ _____

Tax (4.166%) $ _____

Grand Total $ _____

_____ Check Enclosed (payable to Watermark Publishing)

_____ Charge my credit card

____Visa __ Mastercard __ American Express __ Discover

_____ EXP: _____

Signature: _____

Watermark Publishing

1088 Bishop St., Ste. 310
Honolulu, HI 96813
TOLL-FREE: 1-866-900-BOOK • www.bookshawaii.net

CORPORATE DISCOUNTS ARE AVAILABLE FOR BULK PURCHASES.

Please contact us at sales@bookshawaii.net *or* 808-587-7766.